PURR-FECT
Dishes

KEEP

YOUR

Cat

A ♥

KITTY

PURR-FECT
Dishes

Whisker-Licking
♥ *and* ♥
Nutritious
Recipes
♥ *for* ♥
Your Favorite
Feline

♥

TERI GOODMAN

Illustrations by PABLO HAZ

Hearst Books
New York

Grateful thanks to the wonderful team of feline volunteers and their gracious human companions: Joan and Lindsay Corrigan's *Power* and *Taxicat;* Jim Dodge and Frank Lignelli's *Kitty;* O.J. and Gary Shansby's *Caviar;* Lyn Aug Stein and Jay Strickler's *Zippy, Sidney,* and *Osie;* Donia Bijan and Virgil Romua's *Boots,* residing at the Sherman House; Sandra Bendayan and David Ballard's *Catty Watty* and *Harbill;* Ken Grooms's *Tonk;* Kathy, Leslie, and David Manace's *Montrachet;* Sally and Gordon Taubenheim's *Max;* Leslie Gans's *Sam;* Grace Gill's *Amo;* Mary Fong's *Charlie* and *Simon;* Silvia Fernandez and Paul Ash's *Samantha* and *Malcolm;* and, the well-cared-for, but temporarily homeless, kitties at San Francisco's SPCA. In addition I'd like to thank Liz Lawrence and Andy Goodman for their unconditional support and general assistance. For inspiration and invaluable contributions, thanks to Esther Mitgang and Patricia Stapley of Fly Productions. And a very special thank-you to Connie McCole, who introduced me to Fly Productions.

It is the policy of William Morrow and Company, Inc., and its imprints and affiliates, recognizing the importance of preserving what has been written, to print the books we publish on acid-free paper, and we exert our best efforts to that end.

LIBRARY OF CONGRESS CATALOGING-IN-PUBLICATION DATA
Goodman, Teri
    Purr-fect Dishes: whisker-licking and nutritious recipes for your favorite feline/ by Teri Goodman: illustrations by Pablo Haz — 1st ed.
        p. cm
ISBN: 0-688-12813-0
1. Cats — Food — Recipes. I. Title.
SF447.6.G66 1995
636.8'055 — dc20   94-29973
                                    CIP
Printed in the United States of America

FIRST EDITION

1 3 5 7 9 10 8 6 4 2

FLY PRODUCTIONS

for Mom,

♥

who serves a wonderful meal to all species,

♥

feline, human, and otherwise

♥

Contents

Purr-fect Dishes

Introduction

Peple like us, who share our lives with pets, particularly enjoy the nurturing part of the relationship. Feeding is perhaps the most elemental way to nurture the one you love. *Purr-fect Dishes* offers an assortment of main-course meals, a tasty gravy topping (designed to please the cattiest), and a between-meal munchie to cook for your cat. These healthful recipes are *both* delicious and nutritious. ♥ To ensure the wide appeal of each dish, I employed a team of discerning feline volunteers, who taste-tested each recipe. Following their advice, I built the main course meals around liver, poultry, and fish, the three ingredients that the majority favored with a unanimous purr (all excellent sources of protein, too.). To these flavor-favorites, I added healthy bonus ingredients such as bone meal, wheat germ, brewer's yeast, bran, corn oil, garlic, and iodized salt to boost the nutritional value of the meal without compromising the tempting taste. ♥ Cats on healthy diets look better, feel better, and live longer. So, whether you're making your cat's dinner from scratch or serving prepared food, it's worth the extra effort to add these nutritional supplements to your cat's diet to promote bright eyes, strong bones, and shining coats: corn oil and corn oil margarine, high in fatty acids and vitamin E; bran and grains, high in fiber to help kitty digest vegetables and packed with vitamins and minerals such as vitamin A, the B vitamins, and vitamin C; brewer's yeast, an alternative source of all-important protein; wheat germ, loaded with vitamin B; garlic, because cats simply love the flavor, and because, some say, it repels fleas; and bone meal, practically pure calcium, for strong bones. ♥ Cats are creatures of habit and react poorly to change. They can act finicky around mealtime for reasons that have nothing to do with the flavor or the texture of the food. Here are some simple dinnertime rules to improve kitty's table manners: 1. Cats are grazers. They prefer to eat a couple of small meals, rather than one large meal. Feed your cat twice a day, once in the morning and once in the evening. The more small meals the better. 2. Cats are super-sensitive to the amount of food placed in their bowls. An appetizing portion ranges between three and a half and five ounces per serving. All of these recipes yield two portions, except the batch of Shortbread Cookies and the Fish & Garlic Gravy, which yield multiple servings and can be stored for weeks. 3.

Cats like their food served at room temperature and will shun food that is too hot or too cold. 4. Cats prefer fresh food and will turn up their noses at food that has been left out for hours or refrigerated for more than three days. To extend freshness, store leftovers in airtight containers. 5. A bowl of fresh water should be a permanent fixture beside your cat's dish. 6. Set up a feeding schedule and stick to it. ♥ Common sense will tell you what's best for your sweet friend. Before you introduce any new foods or food supplements, check with your vet to determine whether your cat has any health problems that make it necessary to control protein intake or to avoid particular food groups. If your cat is overweight, you should check with your vet about putting kitty on a low-fat diet. Your veterinarian should be consulted before designing an overall nutritional program for your cat. ♥ The more closely we relate to our feline friends, and they to us, the more apparent it becomes that a selfless expression of respect, consideration, and kindness is the key to a happy, healthy, and loving relationship. Cooking a fresh and flavorful meal for your little darling is a wonderful way of showing you care in a language, I feel sure, your cat can understand. I extend best wishes to you and your cat for a long life filled with scrumptious meals and purr-fect health.

CHATCUTERIE GARNIE

Liver Pâté

L iver is definitely a "10" on the Feline Flavor Scale. Happily, it's also an excellent source of protein and vitamin A, both top-priority nutrients in your cat's diet. ♥ Whenever possible, try to mix some bonus ingredients into your kitty's dinner. Here, I add bone meal, a great source of calcium, to make the meal nutritionally complete. ♥ My Chatcuterie Garnie is truly gourmet. Baked French-style in a *bain-marie*, the recipe yields two perfectly cat-size pâtés.

Makes Two Portions (2 Four-Ounce Pâtés)

2 chicken hearts
2 chicken gizzards
6 ounces chicken livers
1 ounce chicken fat
1 large egg
1/2 teaspoon bone meal
1/8 teaspoon garlic powder
1/8 teaspoon iodized salt
Sprig of fresh parsley for garnish

Rinse the chicken hearts, gizzards, and livers under cold water. Pat dry. Dice the hearts and gizzards. Set aside.

Preheat the oven to 350°F.

In a small skillet, render the chicken fat over low heat. It will yield one tablespoon. Transfer the rendered fat to a small bowl and set aside.

In the same skillet, reheat one teaspoon of the reserved fat over medium heat. Add the hearts and gizzards and cook until brown, about two minutes. Remove from the skillet and set aside.

In a food processor, combine the livers, egg, bone meal, garlic powder, and salt. Process until smooth. Add the reserved hearts and gizzards. Process just to combine for a pâté with a chunky, country-style texture.

Prepare two four-ounce mini-loaf pans: Coat each with one teaspoon of the reserved fat. Spoon an equal portion of pâté mixture into each pan.

Bring three cups of water to a boil. Place a nine-inch cake pan in the oven. Fill it with the boiling water. Sit the loaf pans in the water bath and bake for thirty minutes.

Remove the pâtés from the oven and set aside to cool before placing them in the refrigerator to chill firm, about three hours. Return to room temperature before serving. Remove both pâtés from their loaf pans.

To serve, slice one pâté into bite-size morsels and place it in your cat's dish. Top with a crisp sprig of fresh parsley. Place a bowl of fresh water beside the dish. Tightly wrap the second Chatcuterie Garnie loaf in plastic. It will keep in the refrigerator for up to three days. Return to room temperature before serving.

WHISKER LICKIN' HOT POT

Lamb & Olive Couscous

Cats can taste (and enjoy) a complex variety of flavors. Don't hesitate to introduce new foods into your cat's diet. ♥ The carrots, peas, chickpeas, and olives in this recipe offer a wonderful assortment of tastes and textures to delight kitty's little tongue. ♥ Lamb & Olive Couscous is a hearty dish with plenty of energy-packed protein and fiber-rich grain to keep your cat strong and spry.

Makes Two Portions

3 cups chicken stock

1 small lamb shank bone

2 tablespoons diced carrot

2 tablespoons petite peas

1 tablespoon diced cooked chickpeas

1 tablespoon sliced pitted black olives

2 teaspoons corn oil

1 small clove garlic, minced

4 ounces ground lamb

1/4 cup instant couscous

In a heavy-bottomed saucepan, combine two cups of the chicken stock and the lamb bone. Bring to a boil. Lower the heat and simmer, covered, for fifteen minutes. Add the carrots and cook for five minutes. Add the peas, chickpeas, and olives, and cook for two minutes. Remove the lamb bone and set aside to cool to room temperature. Transfer the vegetables to a bowl with a slotted spoon and set aside. Strain the cooking stock into a measuring cup to yield one-half cup of liquid. If there is less, add chicken stock as needed.

Remove any meat from the lamb bone and add it to the vegetable mixture. Discard the bone.

In a heavy-bottomed saucepan, heat the corn oil over medium heat. Add the garlic and sauté for one minute. Add the ground lamb and stir-fry for three minutes. Add the reserved stock and vegetables. Stir well to combine. Bring to a boil. Stir in the couscous and turn off the heat. Allow the couscous to steam, covered, for five minutes, or until it's tender.

My kitty taste testers preferred their Lamb & Olive Couscous best on the soupy side, so feel free to add chicken stock if the couscous is too dry. Set aside to cool to room temperature before serving.

To serve, simply spoon half the couscous into your cat's dish beside a bowl of fresh water. Place the second portion of Whisker Lickin' Hot Pot in an airtight container. It will keep in the refrigerator for up to three days. Return to room temperature before serving.

CATZLBECATZ AZTECA

Chicken With Mole Sauce

Treat your cat to a Mexican-style chicken dinner. The carob in my mole sauce is much healthier for your kitty than the chocolate in classic mole sauce enjoyed by humans. ♥ Cats seem to prefer the dark meat parts of the chicken to the drier white meat of the breast. For best results, use thigh meat in Catzlbecatz Azteca. ♥ Just wait and see, your little friend will lap up the tangy sauce and devour the succulent chicken with gusto.

Makes Two Portions

2 chicken thighs
2 tablespoons corn oil margarine
1 tablespoon all-purpose flour
1/2 cup chicken stock
1 teaspoon finely ground peanuts
1 teaspoon carob powder
1 small clove garlic, minced
1/2 teaspoon soy sauce
1/2 teaspoon honey

Rinse the chicken under cold water. Pat dry.

In a heavy-bottomed skillet, melt the margarine over medium heat. Add the chicken thighs and cook, covered, for ten minutes on each side, or until the chicken is cooked through to the bone. Remove the chicken and set aside to cool to room temperature. Pour off all but two tablespoons of pan drippings.

To make the mole sauce: Turn the heat under the skillet to low and whisk in the flour. Gradually add the chicken stock and cook, stirring, until the roux thickens, about two minutes. Add the peanuts, carob powder, garlic, soy sauce, and honey. Cook, stirring to combine thoroughly, for about three minutes. Transfer to a bowl and set aside to cool to room temperature.

Carve the chicken meat off the bone, discarding the skin if your cat is on a weight-loss diet. Coarsely chop in a food processor or shred into bite-size pieces by hand.

To serve, place half the chicken chunks in your cat's dish. Drizzle half the luscious mole sauce on top. Toss to coat completely. Don't forget the bowl of fresh water. Place the second portion of Catzlbecatz Azteca in an airtight container. It will keep in the refrigerator for up to three days. Return to room temperature before serving.

TARTAN TREATS

Shortbread Cookies

Create a nurturing tradition — share a quiet moment on a lazy afternoon with your best friend. ♥ While you relax with a steaming cup of tea and a buttered scone, your cat will curl up beside you and happily munch a shortbread cookie made especially for him or her. ♥ Not missing an opportunity to provide some valuable nourishment, I make the cookie dough with wheat germ, rich in B vitamins, and bran, which gives the Tartan Treats their crunchy texture. Their sweet flavor comes from cantaloupe, an unusual feline favorite.

Makes Three Dozen Cookies

3 tablespoons butter, chilled
1 tablespoon toasted wheat germ
1 tablespoon bran
1/2 cup unbleached, all-purpose flour
1/8 ripe cantaloupe melon, skinned and seeded
One 10- by 10-inch sheet parchment paper

In a small mixing bowl, combine the butter, wheat germ, and bran. Blend with a fork or metal pastry cutter until well combined. Add the flour, a little at a time, blending to incorporate thoroughly.

Mince the cantaloupe to yield about two tablespoons. Gently pat with a paper towel to absorb the juices. Add the cantaloupe to the flour mixture. Stir to blend thoroughly.

Shape the dough into a ball. Place the ball between two eight-inch squares of waxed paper. Roll out with a rolling pin to form a six-inch square, about one-third-inch thick. Remove the top sheet of waxed paper.

Firmly score the top of the dough with a knife, but don't slice through, to etch a grid pattern of thirty-six one-inch squares. Cover with a sheet of parchment paper. Wrap tightly in plastic or place in an airtight container. Refrigerate the dough for at least one hour before baking.

Preheat the oven to 250°F.

Remove the plastic wrap, if used, and place the cold dough, parchment side down, on an ungreased baking sheet. Remove the waxed paper. Bake in the oven until the shortbread rises slightly and becomes firm, about one hour and thirty minutes. Set aside to cool to room temperature.

The shortbread will easily break apart along the lines of the grid pattern. The Tartan Treats will keep for weeks in a cookie jar, ready to serve at a moment's notice.

BELLE EPOQUE BUFFET

Salmon Quenelles With Shrimp Sauce

D on't let this fancy French presentation fool you. Salmon Quenelles With Shrimp Sauce has all the nutrients your cat needs to keep it bright-eyed and bushy tailed. ♥ The fresh fish is a winning source of protein, iodine, zinc, and vitamin E; the bone meal is practically pure calcium; the brewer's yeast is loaded with B vitamins; and the garlic is believed to ward off fleas. ♥ My team of taste testers was especially intrigued by the creamy-smooth texture of the quenelles and chowed down eagerly.

Makes Two Portions (Ten to Twelve Quenelles)

2-ounce salmon fillet
1 jumbo shrimp, in the shell
1 egg yolk
1 teaspoon butter, softened
Pinch of iodized salt
1/8 teaspoon minced garlic
1/2 teaspoon bone meal
1/2 teaspoon brewer's yeast
1 teaspoon corn oil
1 teaspoon all-purpose flour

Rinse the salmon and shrimp under cold water. Pat dry.

In a food processor, combine the salmon, egg yolk, butter, salt, garlic, bone meal, and brewer's yeast. Process for thirty seconds. Transfer the paste to a bowl, cover, and refrigerate for one hour.

To prepare the quenelles: In a large skillet, bring two cups of water to a simmer over medium heat. Use a wet spoon to scoop out one-half teaspoon of the chilled paste. Use a second wet spoon to gently push the sticky ball into the simmering water. Repeat until all the mixture is used up. (You should have ten to twelve quenelles.) Cover the skillet and poach until they double in size, about four minutes. Remove with a slotted spoon and place on paper towels to drain. Reserve the poaching liquid.

To prepare the shrimp sauce: In a skillet, heat the corn oil over medium heat. Add the shrimp and sauté for forty-five seconds on each side, just until the shrimp turns pink. Set it aside to cool to room temperature.

Shell the shrimp, dice it, and set aside in a small bowl. Discard the shell.

In a small saucepan, combine one tablespoon of the reserved poaching liquid and the flour. Stir to form a smooth paste. Place the saucepan over medium heat and slowly add one-half cup of the remaining poaching liquid, stirring constantly. Cook until the sauce thickens, about three minutes. Add the diced shrimp and stir to coat. Set aside to cool to room temperature.

To serve, slice five or six quenelles into bite-size pieces and place in your kitty's dish. Top with half the shrimp sauce. Place a bowl of fresh water within easy reach. Store the second portion of Belle Epoque Buffet in an airtight container. It will keep in the refrigerator for up to three days. Return to room temperature before serving.

SOUL FOOD DINNER

Giblets & Greens

A cat's sense of well-being is directly related to its state of health. ♥ Nothing is more nutritious for your cat than liver. In fact, many vets believe that cats should eat it twice a week. Cats love its pungent flavor. ♥ Liver combined with robust-flavored chicken giblets and fresh, springy sprouts (my panel of test cats favored alfalfa sprouts) makes Giblets & Greens a soul food dinner for your cat.

Makes Two Portions

4 chicken gizzards

4 chicken hearts

2 ounces chicken livers

3 tablespoons corn oil margarine

1/8 teaspoon garlic powder

1/8 teaspoon iodized salt

1 cup chicken stock

1 tablespoon brewer's yeast

1 tablespoon all-purpose flour

1/4 cup alfalfa sprouts

Rinse the gizzards, hearts, and livers under cold water. Pat dry. Dice the gizzards and hearts.

In a heavy-bottomed skillet, melt one tablespoon of the margarine over medium heat. Add the gizzards, hearts, garlic powder, and salt. Cook, covered, stirring occasionally to prevent sticking until the giblets are browned, about ten minutes. Transfer to a small bowl and set aside to cool to room temperature.

Bring the chicken stock to a boil in a small saucepan.

In the same skillet, melt one tablespoon of the margarine over low heat. Add the livers and cook, covered, for three minutes on each side. Transfer to a food processor. Add the brewer's yeast and process until smooth.

Turn the heat up under the skillet to medium. Add the remaining tablespoon of margarine. Whisk in the flour and cook, stirring constantly, for two minutes. Gradually stir in the boiling stock. Cook, stirring, until the roux thickens, about one minute. Add the liver purée and cook, stirring to combine thoroughly, until the mixture is heated through, about two minutes. Transfer the gravy to a bowl and set aside to cool to room temperature.

To serve, create a bed of half the alfalfa sprouts in the bottom of your cat's dish. Top with half the giblets and crown with half the liver gravy. Place a bowl of fresh water beside the dish. Store the second portion of the giblets and gravy and the second portion of the alfalfa sprouts in separate airtight containers. They will keep in the refrigerator for up to three days. Return the giblets and gravy to room temperature before serving.

Chow Mein

Roast Duck Breast With Lo Mein Noodles

If you've hesitated to serve duck to your cat because it's especially fatty, fear no more. ♥ Cats have a greater need for fat in their diets than humans do. Even so, the richness of the meat should make duck a special-occasion food. ♥ For a lovely, lean-feline Chow Mein, I sear, then roast, then skin the duck breast. I toss in some mushrooms for minerals, add some greens for fiber and texture, and for my trouble, I receive a "standing" ovation from my squad of discerning kitlings.

Makes Two Portions

6-ounce boneless duck breast
1 small clove garlic, minced
2 tablespoons soy sauce
1 teaspoon oyster sauce
1/4 teaspoon sesame oil
1/2 teaspoon corn oil
1/4 cup finely shredded bok choy
1 tablespoon diced mushroom
1 tablespoon minced scallion, white part only
1 ounce fresh lo mein noodles

Rinse the duck breast under cold water.

In a medium bowl, combine the garlic, soy sauce, oyster sauce, and sesame oil. Add the duck breast. Turn to coat. Cover the bowl with plastic wrap. Place in the refrigerator for at least one hour. Turn the breast once or twice to marinate evenly.

Preheat the oven to 375°F.

Remove the duck breast from the marinade and pat dry. Reserve the marinade.

In a heavy-bottomed ovenproof skillet, heat the corn oil over high heat. Add the duck, reduce the heat to medium, and sear for three minutes on each side. Turn off the heat. Remove the breast and pour off all but about one tablespoon of cooking fat. Return the duck to the skillet, skin side up, and drizzle on one tablespoon of the marinade. Place the skillet in the oven. Roast until the breast is cooked tender, about ten minutes. Transfer the breast to a platter to cool to room temperature.

Pour off all but about one tablespoon of cooking fat from the skillet and return to the stove top. Add the bok choy, mushroom, and scallion. Stir-fry over medium heat to wilt the vegetables, about one minute. Transfer to a bowl to cool to room temperature.

Bring a quart of water to a boil in a large pot. Add the noodles and cook until soft, about three minutes. Rinse under cold water and drain. Set aside.

Skin the cooled duck breast. Cut the meat into bite-size pieces. Add the duck meat and the noodles to the bowl of vegetables. Toss thoroughly.

To serve, place half the Chow Mein in your cat's dish beside a bowl of fresh water. Store the second portion in an airtight container. It will keep in the refrigerator for up to three days. Return to room temperature before serving.

BONSAI BOX LUNCH

Broiled Mackerel Maki

Yes, traditional sushi *is* raw and risky, but I broil the mackerel to avoid the chance of contamination from microorganisms that can live in raw fish. ♥ If you've never made a maki roll, you'll be surprised at how simple it is to prepare this Japanese morsel. It's as easy as broiling the fish, boiling the rice, seasoning with a pinch of scallion and a sprinkle of sesame seeds, and then rolling it all up in a sheet of sea-flavored nori. ♥ The Bonsai Box Lunch is a real winner with lots of minerals and cat-friendly nutrients to keep your kitty brainy and beautiful.

Makes Two Portions (Eight Individual Maki)

6-ounce mackerel fillet
3/4 cup bottled clam juice
1/4 cup white rice
1 teaspoon corn oil
2 tablespoons soy sauce
1/2 tablespoon minced scallion
1/2 teaspoon toasted sesame seeds
One 5 1/2- by 7-inch sheet dried nori (Japanese seaweed)

Rinse the mackerel fillet under cold water. Pat dry.

Preheat the broiler.

In a medium saucepan, bring the clam juice and rice to a boil over high heat. Lower the heat and simmer, covered, until the rice is tender, about eighteen minutes. Drain well. Set aside in a bowl to cool to room temperature.

Coat the bottom of a broiling pan with the corn oil. Place the fish, skin side up, in the pan and broil for five minutes. Baste with the soy sauce and continue to broil for five minutes more. It's not necessary to turn the fish. Set aside in the pan to cool to room temperature.

Remove the fish skin and dice. Flake the meat into bite-size pieces. Check the meat carefully to remove pin bones.

Add the fish and skin to the bowl of rice. Pour on the broiling juices. Add the scallion and sesame seeds, and toss to combine thoroughly.

To prepare the nori roll: Place the nori in the broiler, shiny side up. Broil until it turns dark green, about thirty seconds. Transfer the nori to a work surface. Spread the rice mixture in an even layer on top to cover. Leave a one-quarter inch border of uncovered nori around the rice so it doesn't spill out when it's rolled. Start at the bottom, along the shorter edge, and roll upward, tightly, to form a firmly packed seaweed cylinder. Slice the nori roll into eight rounds, about seven-eighths of an inch each.

To serve, place four maki in kitty's bowl and watch the fun as the bite-size morsels disappear in the blink of a cat's eye. Remember to place a bowl of fresh water beside the dish. Store the second portion of Bonsai Box Lunch in an airtight container. It will keep in the refrigerator for up to three days. Return to room temperature before serving.

TASTY TOPPING

Fish & Garlic Gravy

You can rekindle even the most stubborn appetite with the lip-smacking taste of Tasty Topping. I call it sneaky sauce because it contains a bit of every flavor that cats adore — fish, garlic, onion, salt, and the irresistible chicken fat. ♥ It's delicious, it's aromatic, it's healthful, and it'll lure any rebel without a cause back to its bowl of food. ♥ When I used the sauce to dress up a dinner of plain boiled rice, my intrepid band of fearless felines slurped it up zestfully.

Makes Eight Portions (Two Cups of Gravy)

8-ounce tuna fillet
2 ounces chicken fat
1/4 small onion, coarsely chopped
1 small carrot, coarsely chopped
2 sprigs fresh parsley
3 cups water
1/4 teaspoon iodized salt
One 6- by 6-inch piece cheesecloth
2 cloves garlic, thinly sliced

Rinse the fish under cold water. Pat dry.

In a medium heavy-bottomed saucepan, render the chicken fat over low heat. It will yield two tablespoons. Transfer the rendered fat to a small bowl and set aside.

In the same saucepan, reheat one tablespoon of the reserved fat over medium heat. Add the onion, carrot, and parsley. Reduce the heat to low and cook, covered, stirring occasionally, for six minutes. Transfer the vegetables to a bowl and set aside to cool.

In another saucepan, bring the water and salt to a boil.

Place the vegetables in the center of the cheesecloth square. Fold up the sides to make a little pouch. Twist the ends together and tie closed with twine.

In the first saucepan, reheat the remaining rendered chicken fat over medium heat. Add the fish and brown for two minutes on each side. Reduce the heat to low and slowly pour in the boiling salted water. Stir to combine, breaking up the fish and deglazing the bottom of the pan. Add the pouch of vegetables and the garlic. Simmer, covered, for twenty minutes. Set aside to cool to room temperature.

Remove the pouch of vegetables and discard. Transfer the fish mixture to a food processor and process until well combined, about thirty seconds. Strain the gravy through a sieve into a quart-size glass measuring cup. Discard the solids. Set aside to cool to room temperature.

Pour the Tasty Topping into an ice cube tray with eight sections or freeze in eight individual ice cube molds, about three tablespoons of gravy in each. Cover with plastic wrap. Store in the freezer to use as desired. The gravy will keep for months. Return to room temperature before serving.

CATCH OF THE DAY

Crispy Fish Fry

Variety is the best way to make sure your cat eats a balanced diet. ♥ Interested vets claim it's wise to introduce one new food a week to help develop strong bones, sparkling eyes, sweet breath, and a shining coat. ♥ Crispy Fish Fry put this philosophy to the test. The garlic-flavored fish enticed my feline team to eat every bit of the triCAThalon vegetable mixture in Catch Of The Day. Paws up for zucchini, corn, peas, and potatoes.

Makes Two Portions

4-ounce sole fillet

1 tablespoon all-purpose flour

1/8 teaspoon iodized salt

1 tablespoon wheat germ

1 tablespoon bread crumbs

1/8 teaspoon garlic powder

1 large egg

2 tablespoons corn oil

1 tablespoon diced zucchini

1 tablespoon corn kernels

2 tablespoons petite peas

1 tablespoon diced boiled potato

Rinse the sole under cold water. Pat dry.

To prepare the fish for frying: In a small bowl, combine the flour and salt. Mix together thoroughly. In a second bowl, lightly beat the egg. In another small bowl, combine the wheat germ, bread crumbs, and garlic powder. Mix together thoroughly.

Dredge both sides of the fish in the flour mixture. Shake lightly to shed excess flour. Dip the flour-coated fillet into the beaten egg to coat both sides. Dredge in the bread crumb mixture to coat both sides. Shake lightly to shed excess crumbs. Set aside.

In a heavy-bottomed skillet, heat the corn oil over medium heat. Add the fish and brown for two minutes on each side. Transfer the fish to a platter and set aside to cool to room temperature.

Pour the flour mixture into the beaten egg and stir until smooth. Add the zucchini, corn kernels, peas, and diced potato. Toss to coat the vegetables thoroughly.

To the same skillet, add the coated vegetables, plus any extra egg batter. Stir-fry over medium heat for three minutes. Transfer the vegetables to the platter with the fish and set aside to cool to room temperature.

Flake the fish into bite-size pieces and toss to mix with the vegetables.

To serve, place half the fish and vegetable mixture in your cat's dish with a fresh water chaser beside it. Store the second portion of Catch Of The Day in an airtight container. It will keep in the refrigerator for up to three days. Return to room temperature before serving.

TUBERS AND TOM

Turkey Patties In Parchment

In the autumn, turkey and a bounty of tuberous vegetables take their turn at our table. Happily, these hearty-harvest ingredients also fill a proper nutritional place in your pet's diet. ♥ If you're like I am, you love to share human customs with an animal companion. ♥ Turkey and its holiday complement, the earthy family of tubers, are oftentimes overcooked. Since neither species enjoys dry food, cook Tubers And Tom in a parchment package, and puss's Thanksgiving dinner will be as juicy as, if not juicier than, yours.

Makes Two Portions (2 Five-Ounce Patties)

2 teaspoons corn oil

1/2 teaspoon minced onion

1 teaspoon minced garlic

2 ounces turkey liver

1 tablespoon finely chopped red potato

1 tablespoon finely chopped carrot

1 tablespoon finely chopped turnip

1 tablespoon finely chopped leek, white part only

4 ounces ground turkey

Pinch of iodized salt

1/4 cup cooked pearl barley

Two 12- by 16-inch sheets parchment paper

Preheat the oven to 400°F.

In a skillet, heat one teaspoon of the oil over low heat. Add the onion and garlic. Cook until soft, about three minutes. Turn up the heat under the skillet to medium and add the turkey liver. Cook, covered, for about six minutes, turning once after three minutes to brown evenly on both sides. Set aside to cool enough to handle.

Dice the liver and place in a medium bowl. Add the potato, carrot, turnip, leek, and ground turkey. Season with a pinch of salt. Stir to combine. Add the barley to the mixture and stir well to combine the ingredients thoroughly. Divide the mixture in half and shape into two patties. Set aside.

To prepare the parchment packages, fold the sheets in half the long way. Open them up to lay flat. Oil a five-inch area in the center of each. Position the patties about one inch below the centerfolds. Fold down the top half of each sheet to cover the patties and to close the packages. Bring the short ends up and fold over the middle of the packages to seal securely. Don't make your folds too close to the patties, as air needs to circulate for even cooking.

Place the packages on a baking sheet. Bake in the oven until they puff up and turn light brown, about twenty minutes. Remove the packages and set aside until cool enough to handle. Slice one open to allow the steam to escape and the pattie to cool to room temperature. Discard the paper package.

To serve, cut the pattie into cat-size morsels and place in kitty's dish beside a refreshing bowl of water. Store the second package of Tubers And Tom in an airtight container. It will keep in the refrigerator for up to three days. Return to room temperature before serving.

YE OLDE FAVOURITE

Steak & Kidney Pie

hen it's cold outside, warm your cat's tummy with this savory meat pie. ♥ I created this recipe for my neighbor Jim Dodge's special darling, Kitty. ♥ She's a typical finick who rarely finishes her dinner at one sitting. When presented with this hearty fare, she found the flavors so satisfying, she ate every bit, even chasing the last morsels out of the ramekin with her tiny paw. A very cute sight.

Makes Two Portions (2 Four-Ounce Pies)

1 tablespoon plus 2 teaspoons corn oil margarine
2 tablespoons all-purpose flour
1/2 teaspoon garlic powder
4-ounce chuck steak
4-ounces lamb kidneys
2/3 cup plus 2 tablespoons beef stock
1 slice whole-wheat bread

Preheat the oven to 350°F.

Prepare two four-ounce "oven-to-cat" ramekins. Coat each with one-half teaspoon of the margarine.

In a small bowl, combine the flour and garlic powder. Stir together to mix thoroughly.

Slice the steak into bite-size pieces. Rinse the kidneys under cold water and pat dry. Remove any exterior membranes. Cut the kidneys into bite-size pieces.

Dredge the steak and kidneys in the flour mixture. Shake lightly to shed excess flour.

In a heavy-bottomed skillet, melt one tablespoon of the margarine over high heat. When the margarine is bubbling, add the pieces of meat. Stir-fry until nicely browned, about three minutes. Spoon an equal portion of sautéed meat into each ramekin.

Reduce the heat under the skillet to medium and add two-thirds cup of the stock. Stir with a wooden spoon to deglaze the bottom and sides of the pan. Raise the heat to high and bring to a boil.

Pour an equal portion of flavorful stock into each ramekin just to cover the meat. Seal the ramekins with a double layer of aluminum foil, place on a baking sheet and bake for one hour.

To prepare the pie tops: Remove the crusts from the bread. Butter the bread with one-half teaspoon of the remaining margarine. Cut into half-inch squares.

Remove the ramekins from the oven. Raise the heat to 450°F. Top each ramekin with a layer of bread squares, buttered side up, to form a "pie crust." Drizzle one tablespoon of the remaining stock over each. Return the ramekins to the oven and bake, uncovered, until brown, about ten minutes. Set aside to cool to room temperature.

To serve, break open the golden crust of one pie and place in darling's dish. A bowl of fresh water should be close at paw. Tightly wrap the second serving of Ye Olde Favourite in plastic. It will keep in the refrigerator for up to three days. Return to room temperature before serving.

BILLABONG BARBI

Shrimp On Skewers

When you're planning a barbecue, it's a snap to invite your cat to the party. ♥ Since the grill will be fired up anyway, it takes just a little extra time to prepare kitty's meal in advance and grill it alongside yours. ♥ The beckoning aroma of food cooking on glowing coals raises expectations to a feral pitch, but you'll be able to ward off the sulks with the beautifully turned-out Billabong Barbi.

Makes Two Portions

6 ounces medium shrimp, in the shell

18-inch-long metal skewer

1/2 teaspoon minced shallot

2 tablespoons butter, softened

2 tablespoons chopped mushrooms

2 tablespoons corn kernels

2 tablespoons chopped green pepper

1 tablespoon wheat germ

Prepare a bed of coals for grilling.

While the fire is heating, rinse the shrimp under cold water. Pat dry.

Thread the shrimp on the metal skewer. Set aside.

In a small pot, combine the shallot and butter. Place over medium heat and heat to bubbling. Turn the heat to low just to keep the butter liquid.

In a small saucepan, combine the mushrooms, corn, green pepper, and wheat germ. Toss to mix thoroughly. Add one tablespoon of the shallot butter. Toss again to coat.

Place the vegetables in the center of a twelve-inch square of foil, double thickness. Fold the longer sides in on themselves to cover the vegetables. Fold up the shorter sides to tightly seal the package.

When the coals are glowing, grill the vegetables over medium heat until tender, about fifteen minutes. Slice open the package and set aside to cool.

Place the shrimp on the grill and cook over medium heat until opaque, about two minutes on each side. Set aside until cool enough to handle.

Remove the shrimp from the skewer. Shell the shrimp. Discard the shells. Dice the shrimp into bite-size pieces.

In a small bowl, combine the shrimp and the remaining shallot butter. Toss to coat. Add the grilled vegetables. Toss again to mix. Set aside to cool to room temperature.

To serve, place half the Billabong Barbi in your cat's dish beside a bowl of fresh water. Store the second portion in an airtight container. It will keep in the refrigerator for up to three days. return to room temperature before serving.

♥ *felix*
felicitas ♥